FOOTBALL HALL OF **FAMERS**

VINCE LOMBARDI

Greg Roensch

the rosen publishing group's
**rosen
central**

To George Tuma,
outstanding teacher and friend

Published in 2003 by The Rosen Publishing Group, Inc.
29 East 21st Street, New York, NY 10010

First Edition

Library of Congress Cataloging-in-Publication Data

Roensch, Greg.
Vince Lombardi / Greg Roensch.—1st ed.
    p. cm. — (Football hall of famers)
Includes bibliographical references and index.
Summary: A biography of the legendary coach of the Green
Bay Packers and the Washington Redskins, known for his
belief in hard work, discipline, and pride both on and off
the football field.
ISBN 0-8239-3610-4 (lib. bdg.)
1. Lombardi, Vince—Juvenile literature. 2. Football
coaches—United States—Biography—Juvenile literature.
3. Green Bay Packers (Football team)—History—Juvenile
literature. [1. Lombardi, Vince. 2. Football coaches.]
I. Title. II. Series.
GV939.L6 R64 2003
796.332'092—dc21
                                                    2001008073

Manufactured in the United States of America

Contents

Vince Lombardi is often regarded as the greatest football coach ever, leading the Green Bay Packers to victory in five NFL Championships and the first two Super Bowls.

# Introduction

At the end of each grueling season in the National Football League (NFL), the two top teams play one game to decide which is the best football team in the country. The game that decides it all is called the Super Bowl, and each year it is the biggest one-day sporting event on the planet. Winning the Super Bowl is one of the greatest achievements in all of American sports. For the winning team, it means that the players have overcome tremendous adversity. Surpassing all other teams, they have earned the right to call their team the world's best. It is such an overwhelming accomplishment that it can bring football's toughest players to tears.

At the end of the game, as the players celebrate and dance around the field like children, a trophy is awarded to the victors. The Super Bowl trophy is named after one man who stood at the top of professional football like no one before or since. The Super Bowl trophy is named after the legendary coach of the Green Bay Packers, Vince Lombardi.

Vince Lombardi wasn't a head coach in the National Football League for an especially long time. But, in his ten years as a head coach (nine with the Green Bay Packers and one with the Washington Redskins), he set the standard for all other teams by building the Packers into an NFL dynasty. Before he arrived in Green Bay, the Packers were a very bad team. For more than ten years they were so bad that many people questioned why this small Wisconsin town should have a professional football team at all. In professional football's early years, the league had been built upon teams in small Midwestern towns like Green Bay. But by 1960 the league was much different. Those other pioneer teams were long gone. According to the critics, Green Bay's days of football glory were far in the past and it could never again hope to field a team that could compete with teams from New York, Chicago, San Francisco, and other major cities. Vince Lombardi proved the critics wrong.

In the year before Lombardi took control of the franchise, the Packers won only one game. Their pitiful record put yet another exclamation point on the fact that the Packers were a bad franchise, a losing franchise. But when Lombardi stormed into Green Bay in 1959, he showed right away that he wouldn't tolerate losing. From the start, he infused the team and the front office with a winning attitude, and then he backed it up by building a winning team.

In his first year, Lombardi led the Packers to seven wins and five losses. It wasn't a great record, but after so many years of losing, the team finally had a winning record. Moreover, the players looked forward to the next season, feeling that they could win even more games. Indeed, great accomplishments were just around the corner for the Green Bay Packers.

During Lombardi's reign in Green Bay, he led the Packers to six divisional titles, five National Football League championships, and two Super Bowl wins. He transformed this losing franchise into one of the great sports dynasties of all time.

Based on the rapid turnaround of the Packers, it might seem as if success came quickly to Vince Lombardi. It didn't. It took a long time for him to get his chance as a head coach in the National Football League. For many years, he paid his dues as a high school and college coach. Then, when he finally landed a job in the NFL, it wasn't as a head coach, but as an assistant coach for the New York Giants.

Compared to many of his contemporaries, Lombardi always seemed to be a step behind when it came to getting the big job. While others around him were landing college and professional head-coaching jobs, Lombardi was always overlooked. When he finally got an opportunity to lead a professional football team, he didn't waste any time in showing everyone that he was the right person for the

Jubilant Green Bay Packers players hoist coach Vince Lombardi after he led them to a 35–21 victory over the Los Angeles Rams in 1960 for the Western Division title.

job. Lombardi demanded total control of the entire franchise, and he got it. On the football field and off, Lombardi was in charge. This was his big break and he was going to do everything in his power to make sure he didn't fail.

Lombardi's regular-season winning percentage as a head coach in the National Football League is a remarkable .728 (106 wins, 34 losses, and 6 ties). This percentage ranks up there with the all-time great NFL coaching records. Even more impressive, Lombardi always made sure his teams were ready for the biggest games, and in the postseason Lombardi's record was nearly perfect, including blowout wins in the first two Super Bowls. He had a great ability to get his teams ready for the biggest games.

With his success, Lombardi became a national celebrity. But it wasn't just his ability as a coach that attracted people. There was something special about his personality and his philosophy about football and life in general that went beyond the gridiron and struck a chord with the American public. Over thirty years have passed since Vince Lombardi walked the sidelines and barked out commands for the legendary Green Bay Packers of the 1960s, but he is still recognized as one of the greatest coaches of all time. As the ultimate testament to his lasting influence on professional football, each year's Super Bowl winners hold the trophy that bears his name.

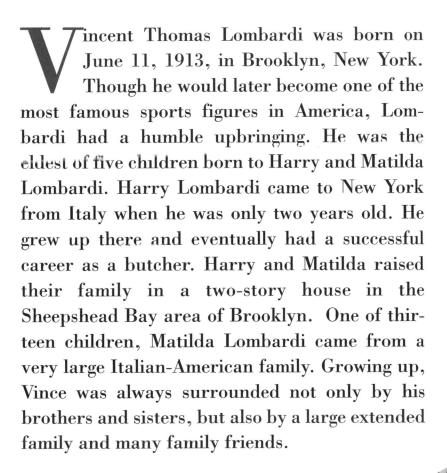

The Early Years

Vincent Thomas Lombardi was born on June 11, 1913, in Brooklyn, New York. Though he would later become one of the most famous sports figures in America, Lombardi had a humble upbringing. He was the eldest of five children born to Harry and Matilda Lombardi. Harry Lombardi came to New York from Italy when he was only two years old. He grew up there and eventually had a successful career as a butcher. Harry and Matilda raised their family in a two-story house in the Sheepshead Bay area of Brooklyn. One of thirteen children, Matilda Lombardi came from a very large Italian-American family. Growing up, Vince was always surrounded not only by his brothers and sisters, but also by a large extended family and many family friends.

Lombardi grew up in the Sheepshead Bay area of Brooklyn, New York, shown above.

At home, young Vince learned the value of hard work and discipline from both his parents. These qualities were also emphasized at school. Brought up as a Catholic and attending Catholic schools throughout his childhood, Lombardi was heavily influenced by religion. In fact, religion was so important to Lombardi that in 1928 he chose to go to high school at the Cathedral College of the Immaculate Conception. He chose this preparatory seminary in Brooklyn because he wanted to study to be a priest. Though his calling later changed to sports rather than the priesthood, Lombardi remained a religious man throughout his life. Even as a busy college and NFL coach, he went to church every morning before practice.

When he became a famous coach in the NFL, Lombardi was known as a stern perfectionist and disciplinarian who challenged his players to be the best they could be. He worked them very hard—pushing them harder than they'd ever worked before—and he expected each player to give his all with no questions asked. Much of Lombardi's strict discipline can be traced back to his upbringing in Sheepshead Bay. Whether he was doing chores at home or helping his father at the meat shop, Lombardi learned from his parents the benefits of working hard and taking pride in any job.

A Different Calling

While studying at Cathedral high school, Lombardi realized that he didn't want to become a priest. Other interests pulled him away. At Cathedral, Vince had participated in sports, including basketball and baseball. But

Cathedral didn't offer—and didn't approve of—contact sports, and that's what really interested Vince. Sometimes, to get his fill of contact sports, Vince would sneak off to a boxing gym. His real interest, however, was football. Vince Lombardi followed football in the sports pages of the newspapers, attended college and professional football games whenever he could, and played pickup football games. He followed the New York Giants professional football team and the great college teams of that era. Eventually, Lombardi gave into the lure of football and left Cathedral.

Lombardi transferred to St. Francis Prep, another Catholic school in Brooklyn. Unlike Cathedral, this school did support a football program. Lombardi received a small scholarship to cover his tuition, and he joined St. Francis for his senior year. Lombardi played the fullback position, and although he didn't have the most talent, he proved to be one of the toughest and hardest-working players. He realized at an early stage of his sports career that talent wasn't everything, and he fully believed that a player who practiced hard and showed a fierce determination could often beat out a more talented player. This was a lesson that Lombardi kept with him throughout his playing and coaching career. Simply put, he was intensely competitive and believed in trying harder than anyone else. During his

Lombardi-Era Packers in the Pro Football Hall of Fame

Vince Lombardi brought out the best in his players, and he had some great ones to work with. These players from Lombardi's Packer teams have been enshrined along with their coach in the Pro Football Hall of Fame in Canton, Ohio:

Herb Adderley	Ray Nitschke
Tony Canadeo	Jim Ringo
Willie Davis	Bart Starr
Forrest Gregg	Jim Taylor
Paul Hornung	Willie Wood
Henry Jordan	

season at St. Francis, Lombardi's team won all but one game. Lombardi played well enough to earn a scholarship to Fordham University, one of New York's leading football colleges.

On the Line

In 1933, Lombardi attended Fordham University for his freshman year of college. Like his previous schools, Fordham was a Catholic school, run by Jesuit priests. As a member of the football team, Lombardi lived on campus. During football season he rose early for a daily regimen of prayer, academics, and football. Even though he was on an athletic scholarship, Lombardi was expected to work as hard in the classroom as he did on the football field. Choosing business administration as his field of study, Lombardi took a rigorous load of classes covering a broad range of subjects. He didn't have it easy just because he was an athlete.

Lombardi came to Fordham as a fullback, but the coaches quickly switched him to the line. At that time, freshmen were not allowed to play varsity football, so Lombardi practiced with the other freshmen, learning the Fordham playbook and scrimmaging against the varsity squad. After one early practice session, the varsity head coach, a man named Sleepy Jim Crowley, moved Lombardi from running back to guard. Crowley figured that Lombardi was too slow for running back, but he also realized that Lombardi was an intense and tough competitor who would be quicker than his bigger opponents on the line. Crowley and the other coaches weren't worried that Lombardi was smaller than the linemen he faced. With speed, timing, and intelligence, Lombardi could beat the bigger players who lined up on the other side of the line. Most important, Lombardi had an intense will to compete and a desire to win that made him succeed even though his opponents were bigger than he was.

When Lombardi was young he had listened to his father tell him that pain was something to ignore. Unfortunately, Lombardi couldn't escape serious injury during much of his time at Fordham. During his sophomore year, he got into some games as a backup lineman, and he

Vince Lombardi won a football scholarship to Fordham University in New York City. In this picture taken around 1935, he shows his legendary intensity while diving for the ball.

even played a little as a starter. For part of the year, however, he couldn't play because he was injured. The following year, he began the season as the starting right guard, but was forced out of the lineup because of injury. Finally, in his senior year Lombardi stayed healthy and remained in the starting lineup for the entire year.

The Fordham team during Lombardi's senior year looked to be the school's best team in years. On the Fordham campus and in the New York newspapers, there was a buzz of excitement about the team. Coach Sleepy Jim Crowley praised his team to one journalist, remarking that the defense was the best he'd ever seen. As the season progressed, the team proved that the attention and praise were warranted. Early in the season, they scored big wins against tough opponents such as Southern Methodist University and St. Mary's. After battling to a scoreless tie against powerful Pitt (the University of Pittsburgh), which included a late goal line stop by Lombardi and his fellow defensive linemen, Fordham looked to be the best unbeaten team in the East. If they could

The Four Horsemen of Notre Dame

Sleepy Jim Crowley was Vince Lombardi's coach at Fordham University. In the 1920s, Crowley was a member of the legendary backfield known as the Four Horsemen of Notre Dame. During a stretch from 1922 to 1924, the Four Horsemen led Notre Dame on an impressive streak in which they won 21 games and lost only one. The 1925 picture below shows all four *(from left to right)*: Don Miller, Elmer Layden, Jim Crowley, and Harry Stuhldreher.

remain undefeated, Fordham would be the eastern representative in the prestigious Rose Bowl in California. It was an exciting time for Lombardi and his teammates.

The Seven Blocks of Granite

A major reason for the Fordham team's success was its core group of excellent linemen. Today, linemen specialize in either offense or defense, but when Lombardi was playing football that wasn't the case. Linemen played both ways and for the entire game. During Lombardi's senior year, as the team rolled on to one impressive victory after another, the New York press became more and more interested in the team and in this group of linemen. In the newspapers, the talented Fordham line were referred to as "the Seven Blocks of Granite," a name that had been used to describe great Fordham lines of the past. On defense, the line was such a dominant force that it was nearly impossible to score a touchdown by running through the Seven Blocks of Granite.

Wall of Granite

The Fordham University line of 1936 led the team to one of its greatest seasons, going 5-1-2 and nearly earning a trip to the Rose Bowl. Allowing just one rushing touchdown during the entire year, it became known as the Seven Blocks of Granite. Lombardi would forever be remembered as a member of those Seven Blocks. The members of the line were Al "Ali Baba" Babartsky, Johnny "Tarzan" Druze, Ed "Devil Doll" Franco, Vince Lombardi, Leo Paquin, Natty Pierce, and Alexander Franklin "Wojy" Wojciechowicz.

With two games remaining in the season the team knew it had a good chance of going to the Rose Bowl. In a game against Georgia, the Fordham team didn't play as well as it could have played, but they still managed to come away with a tie. So, going into the last game of the season,

Fordham's legendary "Seven Blocks of Granite" preparing for a game against Georgia in 1936. From left to right: John "Tarzan" Druze, Al "Ali Baba" Babartsky, Vince Lombardi, Al "Wojy" Wojciechowicz, Nat Pierce, Ed Franco, and Leo Paquin.

Fordham was still undefeated with a 5-0-2 record. A trip to the Rose Bowl would depend on the last game, a tough contest against their bitter rival, New York University (NYU).

In the last game of the previous year, Fordham had dominated NYU 21 to 0 and crushed NYU's Rose Bowl chances. This time, playing at Yankee Stadium in front of about 50,000 fans, the teams would meet to decide if Fordham would represent the East in the Rose Bowl. With such a large reward at stake, the Fordham team played well but not well enough to win. NYU beat Fordham 7–6. As for the mighty Seven Blocks of Granite, they gave up only one rushing touchdown all year, and it came in this game. Fordham finished the year with a 5-1-2 record, but they lost their chance to play in the Rose Bowl. Just like that, Vince Lombardi's college football career was over.

After Fordham

W hat had started out as such a promising season quickly ended in disappointment. The Fordham team during Lombardi's senior year was a very good one, but its loss to NYU was a stinging blow. In one afternoon, the Fordham team's dream of going to the Rose Bowl was wiped out, and Lombardi and his fellow seniors were faced with the realization that they'd lost a great opportunity forever. As quickly as a running back busting through the line for a game-winning touchdown, NYU had captured the day, stomping out Fordham's Rose Bowl hopes in the process.

Along with his teammates and many observers, Lombardi believed that Fordham was a better team than NYU. But, for whatever reason, Fordham wasn't able to win that day. Early in his career Lombardi had learned that he could beat a more talented player if he trained harder, had more determination, and played smarter. From this disappointing loss to NYU, he also learned the hard lesson that on any given day a better team could lose. In any event, Lombardi's college days were soon over, and he needed to find a job.

During the two years after graduation from Fordham, Lombardi searched for a career. He tried a variety of jobs, including working for his father's meat company, but nothing seemed right for him. He also played some minor league football with the Brooklyn Eagles and the Wilmington Clippers. Eventually, Lombardi returned to Fordham to enroll in law school, but that didn't interest him either.

In 1939, he accepted a teaching job at St. Cecilia High School in Englewood, New Jersey. In addition to teaching Latin, physics, and chemistry, Lombardi became the head basketball coach and an assistant coach on the football team. Lombardi had been recommended for the job at St. Cecilia by an old Fordham teammate named Andy Palau. Like Lombardi, Palau had been working at various jobs and playing semi-pro football since graduation from Fordham. When Palau landed the head-coaching job at St. Cecilia, one of his first duties was to find an assistant. Palau had heard that Lombardi might be interested in the job, and soon afterwards Vince Lombardi began his coaching career.

Learning on the Job

Lombardi married his college sweetheart, Marie Planitz, on August 31, 1940. By this time, he had finished his first year as a teacher and coach at St. Cecilia. Showing how competitive he was, Lombardi took on the basketball job with a passion and commitment that would be a trademark of his later success as an NFL head coach. Even though he didn't know much about coaching basketball, Lombardi dove into the job with determination and enthusiasm, working hard to learn the fundamental strategies to build a successful team. In another indication of what was to become one of Lombardi's greatest strengths, he pushed his players to achieve more than they thought they could. During eight years as head coach of St. Cecilia's basketball team, Lombardi's squad developed a winning tradition and even won the state championship.

Though he had success as a basketball coach, football was Lombardi's true passion. During his first season as assistant coach of the football team, the team lost its first two games, but then it rebounded to win the remaining games on the schedule. Lombardi had shown that he was not only a good assistant coach, but that he was also an emotional leader who was able to motivate the team. He could be tough on his players, but he was also fair. He expected his team to be disciplined and he expected his team to work hard. When a player made a mistake, Lombardi made sure the player wouldn't forget it. As he had expected perfection from himself when he was one of the Seven Blocks of Granite, he now expected perfection from his players.

In 1942, Andy Palau left St. Cecilia to return to Fordham as an assistant football coach. Lombardi was promoted to head football

Marie Lombardi said of her husband: "He made football players out of some men. I think he's much more proud that he made men out of some football players."

His experience as a high school coach provided a strong foundation for Vince Lombardi's successful career as an NFL head coach. Here Lombardi is shown riding the practice blocking sled at the Packers training camp in 1967.

coach at St. Cecilia. Prior to Palau's departure, St. Cecilia had been on a successful run, losing only three games in three seasons. Now it was Lombardi's responsibility to continue the success. He brought in new formations and new plays, and he worked the players even harder than before. One of Coach Lombardi's drills was to challenge the players to line up in front of him. He would then challenge them to knock him over. Throughout his career Lombardi believed in challenging his players physically and mentally during practice so that they'd be ready for anything during the game. In fact, his players often commented that the game could sometimes be easy compared to some of Lombardi's practice sessions.

In Lombardi's first game as a head coach, St. Cecilia lost. They didn't lose again that season, however, winning five games and tying two. Pushing harder for perfection the next year, Lombardi coached his squad to an undefeated and untied record. St. Cecilia was in the midst of a 32-game undefeated streak. Even though

The Pro Football Hall of Fame

Located in Canton, Ohio, the Pro Football Hall of Fame is dedicated to recognizing the great players and others who have made the NFL what it is today. At the hall, you can learn about the games, teams, and players who have shaped the NFL. The hall was opened on September 7, 1963.

St. Cecilia was small compared to some of the other schools, it became a dominant football school during Lombardi's time there. This success was due in part to Lombardi's leadership ability. He was a great coach who knew how to get the best out of his players.

But Lombardi was also very successful in another important part of the game. He had a tremendous amount of talent when it came time to evaluate and recruit football players. Just as there was fierce competition between rival schools on the football field each week during the season, there was, in the off-season, an intense battle between schools to recruit players. Lombardi was an excellent judge of talent, and year in and year out he attracted the best football players to St. Cecilia.

Granite Returns to Fordham

When Lombardi played football for Fordham University, the school was one of the nation's football powerhouses. However, times had changed since Lombardi's days at Fordham. During World War II, the school had completely dropped the football program. In 1946, the war was over and football was returning to campus. After his great success at St. Cecilia, Lombardi imagined that he'd be a good candidate for the head-coaching job at his alma mater. As would happen throughout his career, Lombardi was passed over for this job.

The Fordham head-coaching job went to Ed Danowski, another former Fordham player who had gone on to play quarterback for the New York Giants. Fordham didn't win any games in its first year back.

In the second year, Lombardi was hired by the Fordham football team, but not as head coach. He was brought in to coach the freshman football team and to recruit players. Lombardi was undoubtedly disappointed not to get a crack at the head-coaching job, but he couldn't pass up the chance to join a university program. He had done great things at St. Cecilia, but now it was time to move up to the college level.

In 1948, after coaching the freshman team to an undefeated record, Lombardi was promoted to assistant coach on the varsity squad. He was able to turn around an offense that had been horrible for two years. Unfortunately, Lombardi couldn't enjoy his success for long. His ability to succeed with the offense, combined with the team's failure before his arrival, fueled rumors that Lombardi would replace Danowski as head coach. Though the two coaches peacefully settled any issues rising from this, it remained an awkward situation for both of them. Lombardi kept an eye open for jobs elsewhere.

Eventually, he heard about an open assistant-coaching position at the United States Military Academy at West Point. Soon, Lombardi would be on the move to one of the nation's greatest football schools, where he'd be coaching under and learning from Earl "Colonel Red" Blaik. Blaik was considered one of the greatest football coaches in the country.

In the Army

3

ow the parents of two children, Vince and Marie Lombardi moved to the United States Military Academy at West Point in late 1948. If Lombardi had been troubled with the rumors and the conflict surrounding his position as an assistant coach at Fordham, there was no such trouble waiting for him when he arrived at West Point. Colonel Earl Blaik was considered one of the best coaches in the country, and Army was a great team with a great tradition.

Brought in as an assistant coach of the offensive line, Lombardi fit in perfectly with Coach Blaik's system at Army. Blaik was a perfectionist who believed in working hard and preparing the team as much as possible for each

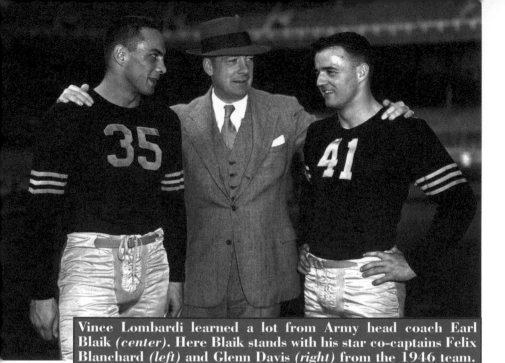

Vince Lombardi learned a lot from Army head coach Earl Blaik *(center)*. Here Blaik stands with his star co-captains Felix Blanchard *(left)* and Glenn Davis *(right)* from the 1946 team.

game. This was nothing new for Lombardi. One of the most important parts of Coach Blaik's preparation was studying game films. Coach Blaik was one of the first coaches to use game films extensively as part of his team's preparation. Each week the Army coaching staff would review footage to discover weaknesses in the opposing team and to come up with strategies to take advantage of those weaknesses. Lombardi quickly saw the benefit of this tool and latched onto studying game footage as an integral part of coaching.

During Lombardi's first year at Army, he had the chance to coach against Fordham. With both teams coming in undefeated, it was shaping up to be a contest between two of the best teams in the East. Fordham had a powerful offense that had been outscoring opponents by a large margin. The game turned into a tough, hard-hitting contest, but the final score wasn't close. Army destroyed Fordham 35–0. For Lombardi and the entire Army team it was a great triumph in a year of great triumphs. Army steamrolled through the season and finished with an undefeated record. In the last game of the season, Army capped off its great year by crushing perennial rival Navy 38–0. After his two disappointing seasons at Fordham, Lombardi had found a home at West Point.

Lombardi's first Army team went undefeated, and he had been a big part of that success. Before his second year, Lombardi was promoted from line coach to coach of the Army offense. Continuing its incredible run of success, the Army team in Lombardi's second season looked to be well on its way to another undefeated season. It rolled through the schedule and had only one team to beat to remain undefeated for the second year in a row.

The season-ending game against Navy looked like it would be an easy win for an Army team that had a 28-0 streak. Unfortunately, Navy turned the tables on Army. For the first time since 1943, Army lost to Navy. The loss was extremely difficult for the Army coaches and players, but by the next season the loss to Navy would seem a small problem compared to other issues facing the Army football team.

A Great Rivalry

The Army team played some memorable games against the Navy team while Vince Lombardi coached at West Point. Like other great college football rivals, these teams placed much more importance on their annual meeting than on any other game. In 1950, for instance, Army was undefeated except for one loss, an upset to Navy. That one loss left a very deep scar on what was otherwise a perfect season.

Nicknamed the Touchdown Twins, Glenn Davis *(left)* and Felix Blanchard *(right)* are widely regarded as the greatest pair of running backs ever to play together on the same college team.

The Scandal

Despite the difficult season-ending loss to Navy, Lombardi's first two years at Army had been good ones. Unfortunately, things were about to change for the worse. As the 1951 season approached, the coaches and the team were looking forward to another great season. However, they soon received word that an academic cheating scandal had broken out at West Point and that many of the football players were involved.

Cheating is a serious matter wherever it occurs, but at a military institution such as West Point cheating is an inexcusable and unpardonable offense. When it was proven that students were passing on answers to exams to other students taking the same test later, it became a huge crisis for the school. Because of the strict code of conduct at West Point, students were guilty not only if they were involved in the cheating itself, but even if they knew about the cheating and failed to report it. After a high-level military investigation, the punishment was announced—ninety students were dismissed

General Douglas MacArthur

An American war hero for his leadership in the Pacific during World War II, General MacArthur was a huge Army football fan. He and Coach Blaik corresponded regularly about the team and other matters. During the Army cheating scandal, when Coach Blaik was considering a variety of options, including leaving the program, General MacArthur encouraged him to stay and rebuild the team.

from the academy. The Army football team was hit extremely hard, losing all but two of its returning juniors and seniors.

The scandal completely depleted the Army football program. In the years leading up to the 1951 season, Army had been a national power. Since 1944, they had compiled an impressive record of 57-3-4. Furthermore, in the year before the scandal, Army had been ranked second nationally, and, with many star players returning to the squad, the team had its sights on a run at a national championship.

Now, as they prepared for a season without their best players, the coaches were faced with the challenge of rebuilding the once-mighty program. After such greatness, and after looking forward to winning a championship, the coaches were faced with the basic problem of just being able to put a team on the field. There was even talk of canceling the season, but Blaik and his coaching staff eventually pieced together a team. Instead of competing for a championship, the squad went 2-7, including a blowout loss to Navy.

After the shock of the scandal and the loss of so many key players settled in, the coaching staff looked at the situation as a challenge and worked hard to rebuild the team. Some people predicted that it would take up to fifteen years for the Army football team to return to greatness after the scandal. In 1952, two years after the scandal, the team took a step toward respectability by completing the year with a 4-4-2 record. Though it wasn't a national championship, it was nevertheless quite a remarkable achievement for a team that had been brought so low. In the following year, the Army team turned it around completely, winning nearly all of its games, including a 20–7 victory over Navy. Lombardi used to tell his players how important it was to get back up after being knocked down. The entire Army team had been knocked down by the scandal, but they were able to rebuild the team faster than anyone had predicted.

Throughout his career at Army, Lombardi learned many things about running a football team from Coach Blaik, and he served for many years as a valuable and loyal assistant. The team had reached great heights and experienced deep lows. Even at the lowest point, with nearly all the starters stripped from the squad, the Army coaching staff got the most out of their players. In a far shorter time than had been predicted the team was able to regain its reputation. Eventually, though, Lombardi felt the urge to move on. After so many years as Blaik's assistant it was time for a new challenge. Lombardi had learned much from his time at Army, but he yearned to be a head coach in charge of his own team.

The Pro Game

When the head-coaching job opened with the National Football League's New York Giants, Vince Lombardi was rumored to be a candidate. One of the owners of the Giants was a man named Wellington Mara. Mara had been Lombardi's classmate at Fordham. It turned out that Mara did want to hire a coach away from the Army staff, but it wasn't Lombardi. Mara wanted to hire Colonel Earl Blaik. Blaik turned down the job, and the head coach position eventually went to Jim Lee Howell. Though Lombardi was passed over for the head-coaching job, he later received an offer to be Howell's assistant coach in charge of the offense. After thinking about the offer and talking to Colonel Blaik about the position,

Lombardi took the job with the New York Giants. It wasn't a head-coaching job, but Lombardi saw it as an opportunity to move up to a new challenge in the NFL.

The Giants had gone through some horrible years. In the year before Lombardi joined the team, the Giants had won only three games. With an ever-enthusiastic Lombardi in charge of the offense and future Dallas Cowboys head coach Tom Landry as the defensive coach, the Giants began to turn things around. At first, Lombardi had to adjust to the pro game and to pro athletes. This was his first experience with professional athletes and it took some time for them to get used to his hard-driving way of coaching. Convincing the pro players that his fiery and disciplined brand of coaching was right for them would take some doing. Over time, though, Lombardi adjusted his football strategies to better suit the bigger and faster players in the professional game. And, as the players began to gain confidence in Lombardi and see positive results in his system, they couldn't argue with his methods.

Tom Landry

After coaching the New York Giants defense, Tom Landry would go on to become head coach of the Dallas Cowboys. As head coaches, Lombardi and Landry would meet as adversaries in many hard-fought football games, including the classic 1967 championship game, known as the Ice Bowl. Landry would eventually win five NFC titles and two Super Bowl championships during his long hall-of-fame career with the Cowboys.

Lombardi *(left)* with Tom Landry

Repetition was one of Lombardi's keys to coaching. In the film room, he believed in watching the same game footage over and over until he understood what every player was doing on every play. He then showed the film to his players so they could see the same things. On the practice field, he believed in repeating plays over and over until a player could do his part in his sleep. You didn't need to learn a lot of plays to run Lombardi's offense, but you did need to know each of the plays perfectly.

One of his favorite plays was the power sweep, which would later become famous in Green Bay as the Packer sweep. Lombardi would make the offense run this play over and over until it was perfect. In this power running play linemen would pull to the side where the ball was being run. Getting out in front of the ball carrier, the mobile linemen would create a wall of blockers who would open holes for the running back. Lombardi instructed the ball carriers to follow the blockers and "run to daylight," which meant that they should look for the best opening and burst through it to gain yardage.

To run the power sweep Lombardi's players had to be precise and quick and smart. Even the big linemen had to have the quickness and agility to get in front of the running back without tripping over their own players or their own feet. Thanks to endless repetition of the power sweep and other plays, the Giants were able to master Lombardi's scheme and ultimately the team became a dominant force in the National Football League.

Giant Success

In Lombardi's first season with the team, the Giants' offense scored over 100 points more than it had the previous year. The team also won four more games than it had the previous year. Though the team didn't have a great record (seven wins, five losses), it was definitely headed in the right direction. Things were looking good for the future. With Lombardi leading the offense and Landry coaching the defense, the Giants had a brilliant one-two punch on their coaching staff. With a high-powered attack featuring Charlie Conerly,

New York Giants quarterback Charlie Conerly *(right)* and halfback Frank Gifford celebrate after beating the Chicago Bears to win the NFL Championship in 1956.

Don Heinrich, Kyle Rote, and Frank Gifford, the Giants quickly became one of the league's best teams. By the 1956 season, Lombardi's third year with New York, the Giants won the title, and his offense was outscoring most other teams in the league. They finished the 1956 season by blowing out the Chicago Bears 47–7 to win the NFL Championship.

After such great success the previous year, the 1957 campaign started strong. However, the team lost its final three games of the year and missed the playoffs. After the season, Lombardi's name surfaced in rumors about vacant head-coaching jobs. The Philadelphia Eagles, then the worst team in the league, offered him their head-coaching position. At first, Lombardi considered taking the job with the Eagles. It was his chance, finally, to run his own team. However, after thinking about it further, and after getting a raise from the Giants, he decided to stay with the New York Giants.

The Giants had another memorable season in 1958. With one game left in the regular season, the Giants trailed the Cleveland Browns by one game in the Eastern Conference. If they could beat the Browns in the final game of the regular season, the Giants would tie for the conference lead and force a playoff to see who would go to the championship game. On a snow-covered field at Yankee Stadium, the Giants and Browns were tied at 10 going into the final minutes. It was a fierce battle that was ultimately decided by a long field goal in extremely poor conditions by Giants kicker Pat Summerall.

After the victory, the Giants were tied in the standings with the Browns. One week later, the same two teams met again in a playoff to decide who would be in the Championship game. This time the Giants defense played a great game, shutting out the Browns and their great hall-of-fame running back Jim Brown. The Giants won 10–0, earning the right to play the Baltimore Colts in the NFL Championship game.

Many football fans still consider the 1958 championship game to be the greatest NFL game of all time. The Colts jumped out to a 14–3 lead at halftime. In the third quarter, the Giants scored a touchdown to close the gap.

After fumbling twice in the first half, the Giants' great running back Frank Gifford made up for it in the second half by catching a pass and running into the end zone for the go-ahead touchdown. With the Giants up by three points late in the game, it looked like they would win the championship. However, in the final minutes, the outstanding Colts quarterback Johnny Unitas rallied his team to a game-tying field goal. Now, in sudden-death overtime, the

Frank Gifford

Frank Gifford was the star running back of Lombardi's offense in New York. An All-American at the University of Southern California, Gifford almost quit professional football after the 1953 season. Instead, with the new coaching staff in place, he stayed with the Giants, thrived in Lombardi's system, and went on to have a hall-of-fame NFL career. After retiring from football, Gifford would have a long career as a part of the *Monday Night Football* broadcast team.

team that scored first would be the NFL champion. The Giants won the coin toss and had the first chance to score, but they couldn't move the ball. In came Unitas, who once again drove the Colts down the field and commanded his team to victory. Though the Giants lost the game, even they had to admit that it was one of the greatest games of all time.

In his five seasons as an assistant coach for the New York Giants, Lombardi had proven that he could excel at the professional level. Yet he was still just an assistant, and he wanted more. He wanted to show everyone that he could succeed as a head coach. So, when the 1958 season ended, Lombardi again listened for offers from other teams. It wouldn't be long before he would find the job he was made for.

5 Green Bay

O n September 27, 1959, the Green Bay
Packers opened the season against the
powerful Chicago Bears, known as the
Monsters of the Midway. Going into the fourth
quarter, the Packers were losing 6–0. Green
Bay couldn't score, and for Packers fans it
looked like it was going to be another losing
start to another losing year. Then, after the
defense recovered a fumble, the Green Bay
offense, led by running backs Jim Taylor and
Paul Hornung, rumbled into the end zone for a
touchdown. After the extra point, the Packers
were only ahead by one point, but that was
enough. The defense capped off the day by
sacking Chicago's quarterback in the end zone
for a safety.

At the age of 45, Lombardi finally got an offer to be head coach of a professional football team. Here, he is all smiles as he packs his bags to take up his new position as general manager and head coach of the Green Bay Packers in 1958.

The Packers, who had only won one game during the entire previous year, started out the new season with an improbable come-from-behind victory over the heavily favored Bears. It was a thrilling victory for the Green Bay Packers and their fans, but it was just a small indication of what was to come under new head coach Vince Lombardi.

Lombardi became head coach of the Packers after the 1958 season. He immediately went to work turning the team around. Even though the team had been terrible the previous year, Lombardi stormed into Green Bay with a positive attitude and a powerful determination to turn the organization around immediately. Before agreeing to become coach of the Green Bay Packers, Lombardi asked for total control of the football operations. He got it. He had complete control of everything on and off the field, from drawing up plays to drafting and trading players. After paying his dues for so many years as an assistant coach, Lombardi let it be known from the beginning that he was in total control.

In Lombardi, the Packers would soon find out they had a coach who would focus his entire being toward making this a winning football organization. No sacrifice was too great for Lombardi. He worked long hours preparing his team, and he expected his coaches and players to show the same commitment to winning. From the beginning he was very demanding of everyone who worked for the Packers, but he was also very demanding of himself.

While some people wondered at first why Green Bay would hire someone without previous head-coaching experience, it became clear soon enough that Lombardi was the right man for this job. He may not have been a head coach of a professional or college team, but his experience had nonetheless prepared him for this job. Because of his slow movement up the ranks, from high school coach at St. Cecilia to college assistant at Fordham and Army to pro assistant with the Giants, Lombardi was fully qualified to handle the duties of the head coach. He wasn't just some young, inexperienced assistant coach looking to make a name

Head coach Lombardi has a laugh with Packers' offensive captain Jim Ringo *(left)* and defensive captain Bill Forester *(center)*.

for himself in Green Bay. Lombardi had been waiting a long time for this opportunity, preparing himself for the day when he could call a team his own.

A New Era

In the early years of the Green Bay franchise, long before Lombardi joined the team, the Packers had won a number of championships, including three in a row from 1929 to 1931. However, by the 1950s the team was in bad shape. There was even talk of doing away with the Green Bay franchise altogether. Lombardi knew that he had his work cut out for him. He realized that the only way to turn around the Packers franchise was to control every aspect of the team. If you were associated with Lombardi's Packers in any way, shape, or form, there was only one way to do things, and that was the Lombardi way. In his first weeks after

The Birth of the Packers

Before there was a National Football League, there was the American Professional Football Association. In 1921, the Green Bay team, which had been sponsored by a meatpacking company, joined the league. In their first game in the league, the Packers played the Minneapolis Marines. Down 6–0 in the fourth quarter, the Packers were led to a 7–6 victory by quarterback Curly Lambeau, who also kicked the winning extra point. As coach of the Packers from 1919 to 1949, Lambeau would win six NFL championships. The current Green Bay Packers now play in a stadium named after him.

signing on as the head coach, Lombardi spent hour upon hour studying films of his team. He watched every game from the previous season, in which the Packers had gone a disastrous 1-10-1. If he didn't know it already, he quickly saw from the film that his task to turn around this football team would not be easy.

One of the first things Lombardi did when he went to work in Green Bay was to redecorate the Packer offices. This symbolized to the staff that things were different now—everything about the team would be new.

From the paint in the office to the attitude of every player on the field, Lombardi wanted to change everything. The previous coach had been easygoing with the players. Lombardi was just the opposite. He instituted rules so the players knew who was in charge. Players had two choices—they could play by his rules, or they could play for another team. When it came to dealing with players, Lombardi showed that he wouldn't tolerate anyone with a bad attitude. One of his first personnel moves was to get rid of one of the star players

Any man's finest hour – his greatest fulfillment to all he holds dear – is that moment when he has worked his heart out in a good cause and lies exhausted on the field of battle – VICTORIOUS

LEAVE
NO REGRETS
ON THE FIELD

Two of Vince Lombardi's sayings hang above the stairway leading to the Green Bay Packers' locker room.

because that player didn't match Lombardi's idea of a team player. The players didn't always like Lombardi's policies, but after they started to get a taste of success they couldn't complain much about his methods.

Lombardi believed in total commitment when it came to football, and he required the same level of commitment from his players. He worked hard, and he expected the players to work hard, too. If they didn't, he yelled at them until they understood what he wanted. He disciplined his team by issuing fines. If a player was late for a practice or missed a curfew, he was fined.

Lombardi also instilled fear in his players by challenging them to prove themselves at each and every practice. He also expected his players to act a certain way in public, making sure that they dressed well and behaved properly when they were on the road. They were expected to act and behave like professionals. If a player didn't want to play by Lombardi's rules, he was released. Lombardi was tough on his players, but he was also fair.

Building a Dynasty

When Lombardi joined the New York Giants as an assistant coach, he turned Frank Gifford from a dissatisfied and underachieving player into a star NFL running back. After a bad season in 1953, Gifford had been ready to leave football, but he decided to give it one more shot with the new coaching staff in place. In Lombardi's offense, Gifford became a major weapon for the Giants' championship teams. When Lombardi

An Explosive Backfield

Green Bay had a powerful backfield combination. Paul Hornung was the NFL Player of the Year in 1960 and 1961. A great player in clutch situations, Hornung was at his best near the goal line and when the game was on the line. Jim Taylor was a tough running back and fierce blocker who rushed for more than 1,000 yards in five straight years. Both running backs excelled in Lombardi's system, and both are now members of the Pro Football Hall of Fame.

came to Green Bay and started studying game films from the previous year, he saw the same kind of potential for greatness in Paul Hornung.

The previous Green Bay coaches had played Hornung at quarterback, fullback, and halfback, but none of the positions was working out for Hornung. Dissatisfied with his performance and tired of two years of losing, Hornung was contemplating leaving football and starting a new career. After one phone call from Lombardi, who informed Hornung that he was going to be the starting halfback, Hornung was ready to give football another chance. Hornung would go on to become one of the league's best players.

Lombardi arrived in Green Bay with approximately six months to get ready for the start of training camp. There was no time to waste in getting ready for the upcoming season. In addition to analyzing game films, Lombardi had to assemble his coaching staff, make many personnel moves to strengthen his team, and do many other things to start turning around the franchise. In May, he held a mini-camp for quarterbacks to explain his offense to them. If the players didn't yet realize that things would be different under Lombardi's regime, they realized it now.

Players who attended those early sessions could see that things would be much different from the easygoing ways of the previous coaching staff. Lombardi brought these players into a room and they studied plays over and over. It was as if they were in a classroom and Lombardi was the teacher. In fact, a key part of Lombardi's success as a coach was that he was an excellent teacher. Lombardi simplified things, getting back to basics and making sure that everyone understood what he was talking about. For many of the players, it was like learning football for the first time. Instead of just ordering players to do things because he said so, he took the time to make sure they understood the reasons behind doing things a particular way. Lombardi believed that if players understood the reason his plays worked they'd be able to execute his plays to perfection.

On the first day of full training camp, Lombardi welcomed his players. Then he told them exactly what to expect. The goal was to build a winning team, a championship team. He had never been affiliated with a loser, he told them, and he wasn't about to start now. He wouldn't tolerate losing, and they shouldn't either. He was going to drive them very hard so that they'd be more prepared physically and mentally than every other team in the league. He was going to make them into the best football players they could be. If anyone had a problem with what he was saying, he told them they could leave right away.

Even though he told them what to expect, none of the players could have been prepared for the intense workouts that were to come. Those who wouldn't push themselves or who didn't have a team attitude weren't Packers for long. Throughout training camp the players were put through an intense training regimen that pushed them beyond what they thought was possible. But it also prepared them like never before for the season.

Vince Lombardi *(left)* transformed Green Bay from a team that was in danger of losing its franchise into one remembered as one of football's greatest dynasties.

As the season approached, many people predicted another last-place finish for the rebuilding Packers. In the preseason, the team won four out of six games. Everyone could see that this was a different team from the Packers of the previous year, who had only won one game. As they began the regular season the players looked forward to the new season with a renewed sense of purpose. Lombardi's work ethic and positive outlook had penetrated the whole team, and they were ready to win.

After the season-opening victory over the Bears, the Packers went on to win their next two games. Winning three in a row to start the season was an outstanding achievement for the Packers, and the press started to take more notice of the team and the new head coach. Following a rough stretch in the middle of the schedule, the Packers finished the season strong with four wins in a row. After winning only one game the previous year, and being picked by so many to finish last again, the Packers finished in third place in their conference with seven wins and five losses.

It wasn't a championship season, but it was the first winning season in Green Bay in over a decade, and Lombardi was named the NFL Coach of the Year. He had succeeded in turning the franchise around and building a strong foundation of players. The entire team could look back on the season with a tremendous amount of pride in its accomplishment. More important, the team looked forward to the next year with high expectations.

The Packer Dynasty

6

At the start of the 1960 season, Lombardi's second with the Packers, the team looked forward to improving their record from the previous year. They had tasted some success, but now they anticipated greater things. Unfortunately, they didn't start very well, losing the first game of the year and then struggling on to a 6-4 record through the first 10 games. The tenth game of the season, however, had been an impressive win over the rival Chicago Bears. The team came together for the stretch run and made it to the playoffs, which culminated in an appearance in the NFL Championship game against the Philadelphia Eagles.

Lombardi often said that his team never lost a football game, but that sometimes time

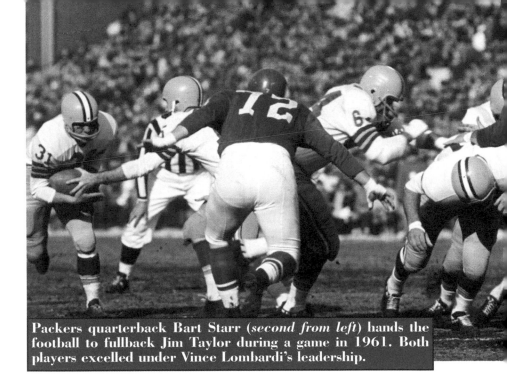

Packers quarterback Bart Starr (*second from left*) hands the football to fullback Jim Taylor during a game in 1961. Both players excelled under Vince Lombardi's leadership.

just ran out. This championship was a tough game, but the Eagles scraped together a 17–13 victory. With Jim Taylor getting tackled just before reaching the end zone on the last play of the game, time ran out on the Packers. Lombardi's team had come up short in its attempt to win a championship, but the coach didn't yell at his players. Instead, he pointed out that it would just be a matter of time until they were back in the championship game. He also told them that they'd never lose another championship game.

One of the major reasons for the Packers' success was the emergence of Bart Starr as starting quarterback. Before Lombardi's arrival, Starr hadn't had much of a career. Mostly he was backup quarterback. When he did get into the game, he was often inconsistent. In 1960, he also began to show flashes of greatness. Even through the tough times, Starr studied the game, and over time he began to show a full understanding of Lombardi's offensive scheme. Just as important, Starr began to develop into a confident and effective team leader. With a new and improved Starr in charge, the Green Bay offense began to hit on all cylinders. Though Starr couldn't quite lead the Packers to victory in the 1960 championship game, he would get more chances to prove his greatness during his career with the Packers.

In 1961, the Packers put it all together, winning 11 games against three losses. In the 1961 title game, the Packers were pitted against Lombardi's former team, the New York Giants. Remembering the loss in the previous year's championship game, and Lombardi's

Bart Starr

The Green Bay Packers drafted Bart Starr in 1956 in the seventeenth round of the NFL Draft. Over time he would become not only a great football player but also a great team leader. Under his leadership during the Lombardi years, the Packers won five NFL titles and the first two Super Bowls. In 1966, he was the MVP (Most Valuable Player) of the NFL. A great player in big games, Bart Starr was the MVP in Super Bowl I and Super Bowl II. He was enshrined in the Pro Football Hall of Fame in 1977.

Vince Lombardi looks on as Bart Starr holds the ball for Jerry Kramer on the eve of their 1962 NFL championship game against the New York Giants. The Packers won 16–7.

earlier promise to his team that they'd never lose another one, the Packers had plenty of incentive to win this game. With the defense rising to the occasion and Bart Starr passing for three touchdowns, the Packers destroyed New York 37–0. The long-suffering Green Bay fans celebrated the victory by tearing down the goalposts. Green Bay, Wisconsin, had become Titletown, U.S.A.

For Lombardi, the win over New York in the title game was a sweet victory, but immediately he was looking forward to the next year and to the challenge of repeating as champions. He praised his players for a job well done, but he also let them know the opposition would try harder to bring them down— everyone would be trying even harder to knock out the champion. Lombardi's goal when he joined the Packers was not just to win one championship. He wanted to create a sports dynasty similar to the great New York Yankees teams. One championship wasn't enough for Lombardi—he had his sights on the ultimate goal every year.

In 1962, the Packers were even better than in the previous year. Pushed more than ever by Lombardi, they won nearly every game during the season, going 13-1. Once again they met the New York Giants in the title game. This time the score was closer (16–7), but the result was the same. Green Bay once again finished the year at the top of the football world. The Packers were clearly recognized as the best team in the NFL, and Lombardi was without a doubt the league's best coach. Winning was now expected in Green Bay. Lombardi never let the team forget this. The more the team won, the more he pushed it toward even greater achievements.

Trouble in Titletown

In 1963, the Packers and Vince Lombardi were dealt a serious blow. It had been reported that some NFL players were betting on football games, which was against league rules. Among the players at the center of the scandal was one of Lombardi's favorites, Paul Hornung. After an investigation, the commissioner handed down the punishment. Hornung, a key weapon

Vince Lombardi poses with the wives of the Green Bay players, who are all wearing mink stoles he gave them after the team won the NFL Championship in 1962.

Vince Lombardi at a press conference after the NFL suspended his star halfback Paul Hornung in 1963. Lombardi told reporters he "would be a fool" if he said the loss didn't hurt.

in the Packer attack, was dealt an indefinite suspension. Lombardi now had to replace one of the team's best players.

Though the scandal was not as large as the cheating scandal at West Point, it was still a huge blow to Lombardi. Like Colonel Blaik leading his Army team back to respectability, Lombardi now faced the task of preparing for the coming season without a key member of the team. After two straight championships, the other teams would be going after the Packers harder than ever. The Packers were able to overcome this adversity, losing only two games during the regular season. Unfortunately, both losses were to the Chicago Bears, so the Packers came in second place to the Bears.

The Packers overcame a serious challenge to put together a great season, but their streak of championships was broken. As proud as Lombardi was of the team, he never took any satisfaction in finishing in any place other than first. Still, there was hope for the future. The team was still a good one, and Lombardi had hope that Hornung would be allowed back into the league for the 1964 season.

Back on Top

Hornung was allowed to rejoin the team for the following season. Though he did a remarkable job of coming back after an entire year away from football, it wasn't enough to bring the Packers another championship. Green Bay once again finished in second place. With an 8-5-1 record, it seemed as if Green Bay's era of dominance was over. After winning the championship in 1961 and 1962, the Packers had now missed the playoffs two years in a row. They were still a good team, but they were no longer viewed as a great team. Little could anyone imagine that Lombardi's Packers were about to go on to even loftier accomplishments.

In 1965, Green Bay tied Baltimore at the end of the regular season. With identical records of 10-3-1, the Packers and Colts met in a playoff game to decide who would play against the Cleveland Browns for the championship. The game was held in Green Bay in harsh winter conditions. The Colts were leading 10–7 with less than two minutes left in regulation time when Packers kicker Don Chandler booted a field goal to tie the game. After ending the season in a tie, these two teams ended the regulation period in a tie score. In sudden-death overtime both teams had chances to win. After nearly fourteen minutes of play in overtime, Chandler was called upon again. He converted a kick from the 18-yard line to win the game for the Packers. After two years away from the playoffs, the Packers were on their way back to the championship game.

Vince Lombardi with star kicker Don Chandler in 1965. Lombardi was tough on his players, but he also knew how to celebrate after a big win.

The Packers met the Cleveland Browns for the 1965 NFL championship game. The turf at the Packers' stadium, Lambeau Field, was a muddy mess, with snow and rain falling on the field before and during the game. The Browns had a powerful offense, featuring Jim Brown, one of the most dangerous running backs ever to play the game. On this muddy day, however, it was the Green Bay defense that stifled the Browns' powerful attack.

On offense for Green Bay, Hornung and Taylor both had great games, with the two of them combining for over 200 rushing yards. The Packers prevailed, scoring a 23–12 victory for the team's third championship in five years. Anyone who thought the Packers were too old to win another championship had to admit that Green Bay was still a great team. It was true that many of the key stars from the earlier championship teams were getting older, but Lombardi was also very smart about evaluating talent. He knew when it was time to bring in younger players to replace or complement the older guys. More important, he knew how to motivate and condition all of his players, young and old, to get the most out of them. In this game against the Browns, for instance, Hornung and Taylor were both nearing the ends of their careers, but they were still able to play a great game when it really counted.

The Super Bowl

The following year, in the 1966 NFL Championship game, the Packers won a very close contest against the Dallas Cowboys. Until that year, the season would have been over after the championship game. This year, though, the league added another game, which would pit the NFL champion against the champion of the younger American Football League. This new game was called the Super Bowl. In Super Bowl I, Lombardi's Packers played against the Kansas City Chiefs.

Max McGee had been a wide receiver with the Packers since before Lombardi had taken over the team. Over the years, McGee had been a leader on the team, but by 1966 his career was winding down. Because of an injury to the regular receiver, McGee got a chance to play in Super Bowl I. After catching only a handful of passes all year, McGee suddenly became one of the biggest stars of the first Super Bowl, by hauling in seven receptions for 138 yards and two touchdowns.

The game was surprisingly close at half-time, but then Green Bay dominated the second half and ran away with a 35–10 victory. For the second time since he'd come to Green Bay, Vince Lombardi had led his players to back-to-back championships.

STARR

LOMBARDI

BOWL

NFL

REEN BAY

The first ever Super Bowl was held in 1967. This promotional poster features coaches Hank Stram and Vince Lombardi and the two quarterbacks, Len Dawson and Bart Starr.

In 1967, the critics were getting louder and louder in saying that the Packers were too old to win another championship. The team had a good regular season, but they were beatable. One of their hardest losses during the season had come against the Los Angeles Rams. In the first round of the playoffs, the Packers prepared to meet the Rams for a rematch. Critics predicted that the Packer dynasty was about to be trampled by the hungry Rams.

In the playoff game, the Rams jumped out to a 7–0 lead, and the critics got even louder, saying that the Packers were too old. After getting the early lead, the Rams were shut out the rest of the way by a suffocating Green Bay defense. The Packers won the game 28–7. As a reward for beating the Rams, the Packers next played the Dallas Cowboys. Again, the critics started saying that the Packers were too old to beat the Cowboys, who were eager to avenge their loss to the Packers in the championship game of the previous year.

On the morning of the championship game in Green Bay, the temperature was nearly 20

The Vince Lombardi Super Bowl Trophy. Lombardi led the Packers to victory in the first two Super Bowl championships. After his death in 1970, the trophy was named after him.

degrees below zero. In the freezing cold, the Packers jumped out to a 14–0 lead early in the game. It looked like the Packers—along with the foul weather—would be too much to handle for the Cowboys. Late in the first half, however, the Cowboys took advantage of critical Green Bay mistakes to score 10 points before the break.

In the third quarter, Dallas took the lead, and it looked like the clock was running down on the mighty Green Bay dynasty. With a handful of minutes remaining in the game, Bart Starr coolly led the Packers down the field. As time was running out and without any time-outs remaining, Starr followed his line into the end zone for the game-winning touchdown. The frozen fans—and players—of Green Bay went wild. This game is now referred to as the Ice Bowl, and it is considered by many to be one of the greatest professional football games of all time. By winning the Ice Bowl, Green Bay earned a right to return to the Super Bowl.

The Packers met the Oakland Raiders in Super Bowl II. At halftime, with the score still close, a group of Packers veterans urged on the team to win the game for Coach Lombardi. Rumors had been circulating that Lombardi was going to retire at the end of the season. If the rumors were true, then the players didn't

The Ice Bowl: December 31, 1967

With the temperature dropping below zero and a minus 46 wind chill factor, the Packers and Dallas Cowboys met at Lambeau Field in the 1967 championship game. Featuring great plays and courageous performances by both teams, it took an incredible drive in the final seconds for the Packers to come from behind and beat the Cowboys. But the most memorable thing about the event was the weather and how both teams staged such a tremendous game in such abominable conditions. With temperatures dropping far below zero on the frozen Lambeau Field turf, the game was a fight for survival and for the NFL championship.

The Packers carry Vince Lombardi off the field after winning Super Bowl II in 1968. They beat the Oakland Raiders 33–14.

want their great coach to go out with a loss. The Packers took control in the second half and beat the Raiders 33–14. This win gave the Packers a record three straight championships.

Soon after the season was over, Lombardi announced that he was stepping down as coach of the Packers. He would remain as general manager, but he had coached his last game for the Packers. It was the end of an incredible run. Nine years earlier, after the loss in the 1960 championship game, Lombardi had promised his team that they'd be back. He also guaranteed that they would never lose another championship game. He was right about both things. Since that loss the Packers had gone on a tremendous run, becoming one of the great dynasties in the history of American sports.

An Abrupt End

Vince Lombardi was born to be a football coach. After stepping down as head coach of the Packers, he worked for one season as general manager of the Packers, but he realized that he missed coaching. When the season ended, Lombardi left the Packers to become head coach of the struggling Washington Redskins.

As he did when he joined Green Bay, Lombardi poured all of his energy into turning his new team around. The Redskins hadn't had a winning season in many years, and the team hadn't won a championship since 1942. Lombardi quickly put his plan into place to build a winning franchise. Incredibly, the Redskins started to win, and early in the season they moved into first place. Lombardi was once again working his coaching magic. The team

Lombardi loved challenges, and in 1969 he took on the daunting task of transforming the Washington Redskins into a winning team.

hit a rough stretch in the middle of the season and didn't make the playoffs. Still, just finishing the regular season with a winning record was a great accomplishment for this team. Lombardi was leading the Redskins in the right direction, and it looked like it would only be a matter of time before the team become another Lombardi-led dynasty.

Unfortunately, this wasn't to be the case. While preparing for the next season, Lombardi began to feel ill. He was diagnosed with cancer. During treatment, doctors discovered that the

Motivational Speaker

Vince Lombardi's coaching philosophy struck a chord in American society that went deeper than just football. For example, businessmen eager to bring Lombardi's winning ways into their business or industry learned lessons from Lombardi on a wide range of topics, such as preparation, discipline, leadership, and teamwork.

Pallbearers carry Vince Lombardi's funeral casket into St. Patrick's Cathedral in New York City.

disease was spreading very fast and he was in the terminal stages. On September 3, 1970, Vince Lombardi passed away. He was fifty-seven.

The football world mourned the loss of its greatest coach. Many of his players attended the funeral services at St. Patrick's Cathedral in New York City. The players he yelled at, swore at, pushed, and fined remembered Lombardi as a tough, demanding coach, but they also realized that he made them better players than they ever could have been without him. He was a truly great coach.

Marie Lombardi looks at the bust of Green Bay fullback Jim Taylor at his induction ceremony into the NFL Hall of Fame in 1976.

It has been over thirty years since Vince Lombardi's death, but his influence on professional football lives on. Other great football dynasties have come and gone, but all dynasties are measured against the accomplishments of the great Packers teams of the 1960s. Over the years, other coaches have tried to imitate Lombardi's coaching drills, his intensity, and his willingness to give everything of himself to get everything out of his players. While his methods can be duplicated, his spirit cannot. He was a unique leader who led his teams to an unmatched level of greatness.

In 1971, as a lasting tribute to Lombardi and in appreciation for his tremendous influence on the game, NFL commissioner Pete Rozelle announced that the Super Bowl Trophy would be renamed the Vince Lombardi Super Bowl Trophy. It was a great and fitting tribute to the coach who led his team to victory in the first two Super Bowls and who always refused to accept anything less than first place.

Timeline

June 11, 1913 Vincent Thomas Lombardi born in Brooklyn, New York City.

1933–1937 Attends Fordham University in New York City.

1939 Begins teaching and coaching at St. Cecilia High School in Englewood, New Jersey.

1947–1948 Assistant coach at Fordham.

1949–1953 Assistant coach at United States Military Academy at West Point.

1954–1958 Assistant coach for New York Giants.

1959 First year as head coach and general manager of the Green Bay Packers. Named coach of the year after his first year.

December 26, 1960 Packers lose championship game to Philadelphia Eagles.

December 31, 1961 Packers win championship game against New York Giants.

December 30, 1962 Packers win championship game against New York Giants.

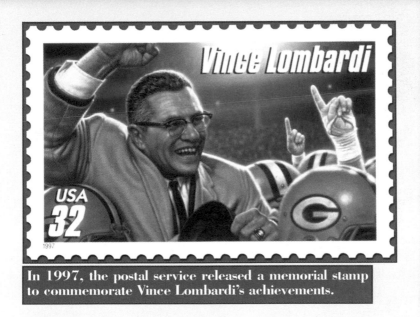

In 1997, the postal service released a memorial stamp to commemorate Vince Lombardi's achievements.

January 2, 1966 Packers win championship game against Cleveland Browns.

January 15, 1967 Packers win Super Bowl I against Kansas City Chiefs.

January 14, 1968 Packers win Super Bowl II against Oakland Raiders.

1968 Retires as Green Bay head coach, but remains as general manager.

1969 Becomes head coach, general manager, and part owner of the Washington Redskins.

September 3, 1970 Lombardi dies.

1971 Inducted into the Football Hall of Fame. Super Bowl Trophy renamed the Vince Lombardi Super Bowl Trophy.

Glossary

AFL The American Football League.

end zone The area between the end line and the goal line.

formation The starting point for the teams.

franchise A team.

gridiron Another name for a football field.

NFL The National Football League.

sack Tackling the quarterback before he can throw a pass.

scrimmage A practice in which offense and defense face each other as if playing a game.

safety Forcing the offense to down the ball in their own end zone.

seminary School for the training of priesthood.

sudden death An extra play to determine the winner of a tied game.

the Sweep One of Lombardi's favorite plays, this running play requires the linemen to be mobile and quick and the ball carrier to be powerful and smart.

For More Information

Green Bay Packer Hall of Fame
855 Lombardi Avenue
P.O. Box 10567
Green Bay, WI 54307
(888) 4GB-PACK (442-7225)
Web site: http://www.packerhalloffame.com

The Green Bay Packers
P.O. Box 10628
Green Bay, WI 54307
Web site: http://www.packers.com

The Pro Football Hall of Fame
2121 George Halas Drive NW
Canton, OH 44708
(330) 456-8207
Web site: http://www.profootballhof.com

Web Sites

Due to the changing nature of Internet links, the Rosen Publishing Group, Inc., has developed an online list of Web sites related to the subject of this book. This site is updated regularly. Please use this link to access the list:

http://www.rosenlinks.com/fhf/vlom/

Video

The Ice Bowl (from The NFL's Greatest Games series). Copyright © 1997 NFL Films, Inc.

For Further Reading

Korth, Todd. *Greatest Moments in Green Bay Packers Football History*. Lenexa, KS: Addax Publishing Group, 1998.

Lombardi, Vince, and W.C. Heinz. *Run to Daylight!* Englewood Cliffs, NJ: Prentice-Hall, 1963.

Maraniss, David. *When Pride Still Mattered: A Life of Vince Lombardi*. New York: Simon & Schuster, 1999.

Wells, Robert W. *Lombardi: His Life and Times*. Madison, WI: Prairie Oak Press, 1997.

Bibliography

Biever, Vernon J. *The Glory of Titletown: The Classic Green Bay Packers Photography of Vernon J. Biever*. Dallas, TX: Taylor Publishing Company, 1997.

Gifford, Frank, and Harry Waters Jr. *Gifford: The Whole Ten Yards*. New York: Ballantine Books, 1994.

Gruver, Ed. *The Ice Bowl: The Cold Truth About Football's Most Unforgettable Game*. New York: McBooks Press, 1997.

Kramer, Jerry, ed. *Lombardi: Winning is the Only Thing*. New York: World Publishing Company, 1970.

Kramer, Jerry, with Dick Schaap. *Instant Replay: The Green Bay Diary of Jerry Kramer*. New York: New American Library, Inc., 1968.

O'Brien, Michael O. *Vince: A Personal Biography of Vince Lombardi*. New York: William Morrow & Co., 1987.

Phillips, Donald T. *Run to Win: Vince Lombardi on Coaching and Leadership*. New York: St. Martin's Press, 2001.

Plimpton, George. *Paper Lion*. New York: Harper & Row Publishers, Inc., 1956.

Starr, Bart, with Murray Olderman. *Starr: My Life in Football*. New York: William Morrow & Co., 1987.

Index

About the Author

Greg Roensch is a writer who lives in San Francisco, California.

Photo Credits

Cover, pp. 9, 24–25, 31, 49, 52, 58, 61, 77, 78, 82, 85, 88–89, 96–97, 99, 100 © Bettmann/Corbis; pp. 4, 70–71, 81 © George Silk/Timepix; p. 12 © Ralph Morse/Timepix; pp. 18–19 © Hulton/ Archive by Getty Images; pp. 21, 32, 38, 41, 43, 91, 94 © AP/Wide World Photos; p. 64 © Vernon J. Biever/Timepix; p. 75 © Wally McNamee/ Corbis; p. 103 © Timepix.

Series Design and Layout

Tahara Hasan

Editor

Christine Poolos